Everything You Need To Know About
STEPFAMILIES

The new members of a stepfamily often feel strange. They need time to adjust.

Everything You Need To Know About

STEP-
FAMILIES

Bruce Glassman

Series Editor: Evan Stark, Ph.D.

THE ROSEN PUBLISHING GROUP, INC.
NEW YORK

Published in 1988 by The Rosen Publishing Group, Inc
29 East 21st Street, New York City, New York 10010

Second printing
Copyright 1988 by The Rosen Publishing Group, Inc

Manufactured in the United States of America

Library of Congress Cataloging-in-Publication Data

Glassman, Bruce
    Everything you need to know about step-families.
    (The Need to know library)
    Bibliography: p. 62
    Includes index.
    Summary: Discusses the problems and adjustments
involved in having only one parent in the family and
what happens when that parent remarries, giving the
child a stepfamily.
    1. Stepfamilies—United States—Juvenile literature.
2. Children of single parents—United States—Juvenile
literature. [1. Stepfamilies. 2. Single-parent family.
3. Remarriage] I. Title.   II. Series.
HQ759.92.G57   1988   306.8'74   88-24022
ISBN 0-8239-0815-1

Contents

Introduction

Sometimes new people join a family. When that happens, a stepfamily is formed. Often it happens when people marry again after a divorce or a death. Then a family gets a new parent. Or a family might get both a new parent and a new child. This new family is called a stepfamily.

Many people think of stepfamilies as being bad. That is a shame. But it is easy to see why they do. Children often believe that "something is wrong" with stepfamilies and stepparents. Even fairy tales give that message. In "Cinderella" the stepmother is "wicked" and cruel. Many children have read "Cinderella." It is easy to see why they think stepfamilies are bad.

Stepfamilies are not new. Even the Pilgrims accepted remarriage. Some of our country's greatest leaders were in stepfamilies. Did you know that George Washington had two stepchildren? Did you know that Abraham Lincoln had a stepmother and three stepbrothers and sisters?

Today there are more stepfamilies than ever. People now can see that stepfamilies are not bad at all. Many studies have been made on the subject in the United States. They show that living in stepfamilies is not "worse" than living in other families. It is just different. Stepfamilies have special weaknesses. But they also have special strengths.

This book will explain the different kinds of stepfamilies. It will discuss family groupings that are common today. It will also discuss the special problems of each of these groupings.

The book also looks at what people expect of each other. Parents and children expect many things from stepfamilies. Problems often arise because of unfair expectations. Most people do not know what is fair to expect of a stepfamily. Family members may want things to be perfect too soon. Then they become upset when small problems come up.

Stepfamilies must be expected to have strengths *and* weaknesses. A stepfamily can grow to be very warm and caring. The love between members of a new family can be very strong. It can be even greater than any love in the family before.

A child and a single parent may grow closer.

Chapter 1

The Single-parent Family

A stepfamily is often created after a child has lived in a single-parent family for a while. Then the parent marries again and the parent and the child enter a two-parent stepfamily. Here are some things that may make that hard:

○ You and your parent have become closer in a crisis.

A death or a divorce is a painful time for everyone. You and your single parent will feel very close after such a crisis. You will have helped each other cope with it. That creates a special bond between you. But then a stepparent comes along. You may not welcome him or her. You may see a stepparent as a threat to your special bond. You may be afraid your special relationship will end. And you would rather live only with your natural parent.

○ You have had all the attention.
In a single-parent family you receive all the attention of your parent. Your parent may not be dating anyone. All his or her free time and energy are devoted to you. Sometimes you even take the place of the missing husband or wife for a while. You and your parent are companions. When a stepfamily is created, the new stepparent needs attention too. That's when you lose the complete attention of your natural parent. And you may feel rejected by that parent.

○ You have adjusted to a single-parent home.
You and your parent can soon adjust to a single-parent family. It does not seem so bad. You get used to new living patterns. You accept new routines. And you may think that two parents are not really needed. But you often forget the needs of your parent. Your parent still needs adult companionship. And she or he may want a sexual relationship. These needs cannot be filled by you. They can only be met by another adult.

Dealing with Mom's Boyfriends or Dad's Girlfriends

A divorce or a death is very painful for a parent. It may make your parent frightened and unsure of what to do. He or she may have many doubts.

Time is needed to mourn (to feel sad about a death). Time is needed to deal with anger before a parent is ready to "enter the world again."

After a divorce your parent must deal with feelings of having failed. The failure of a marriage is a personal thing. After a death your parent must deal with great pain. And great loss.

When time has passed, your parent can feel confident about life again. He or she can look to the future again. Now it is time to go on with life. To pick up where he or she left off. Your parent wants to feel attractive again. He or she wants to feel interesting to other people. To feel appreciated by other adults. This takes much courage. It is very hard to enter the world again.

During this time your parent may start dating. He or she may bring home boyfriends or girlfriends. You probably won't like that. You may have trouble adjusting to these new people. You may have many confusing feelings.

○ "It'll Never Last."

Dear Diary,
Dad just came home with a new girlfriend. I hated her. She looked stupid. She dressed like someone my age. She acted stupid. She smiled too much. She tried to talk to me. She's a teacher and she spoke to me about the students in her high school who are my age. I guess she was trying to be nice but why bother, I'll probably never see her again.

Jennifer, age 15

You may often appear not to care about your parent's boyfriends or girlfriends. There is a reason for that. You do not trust that you will ever see the person again. One of your parents is already gone. It may now be hard for you to believe that anything will last. So you may decide not to care. And you will not try to get to know your parent's friends.

○ Is It Perfect Yet?

Dear Diary,
I really like Mike. He's Mom's new boyfriend. They've gone on three dates already. He has two children. I hope they get married. He wants to take all of us to the amusement park one day. He's good-looking too. He says he has a nice house. Maybe we can move into it. I hope it's soon. I can't wait to have a real family again.

Tanya, age 14

You may want your parent to find another person right away. You may be eager to have a "whole family" again. But you may be expecting too much. You may expect things to go much faster than they can. Then you are disappointed. And then you become angry. You can avoid that. You just need to be patient. You need to give your parent time. You need to have fair expectations.

Children have to understand that their single parents need to meet new people.

○ A Parent "In Love": Yuuucchh!

Dear Diary,
I am gonna barf. Mom has a boyfriend. His name is Lewis. I saw them in the living room. They were holding hands. And kissing. They looked so stupid. I wish they would not do that. Not in the house. I do not want to see it. Mom should not do that. She's too old. She should just forget about boyfriends.

Juan, age 13

Seeing your parent "in love" may make you feel sick. It probably embarrasses you. Especially when you see your parent giggling with a lover or a date. Or flirting and holding hands. That's embarrassing too. And it's hard to get used to. Probably you have never seen your parent acting this way. It wasn't like this with your natural parents.

Remarriage can be difficult for the children. Even the wedding may not seem to be a happy time.

Chapter 2

Becoming a Stepfamily

Why does a parent marry again? All adults need companionship. They need a stable life. They need a sexual life. They also need to have a safe home for their children. That is often what they want the most.

Remarriage Causes Some Confusing Feelings

Remarriage should be a very happy time for your parent. But it is also a difficult time. It is a time of new love. And new hope. But remarriage can be a terrible time for you. Even the wedding ceremony can bring some problems. It means meeting a new family. It means your other parent is not at the celebration. It is supposed to be such a happy time. But it often seems to come at a bad time. It may seem to come too soon after a divorce. Or too soon after a death. You may not be ready. You may feel angry and unhappy. That is very hard to deal with when others are celebrating. No one likes to feel sad when others are happy.

Remarriage often does not allow time for children to show their true feelings. Other people are often too wrapped up in their own feelings to pay attention to you. That can hurt. It is another reason why remarriage can be a difficult time for you.

Two things are very important for any family. One is *cooperation*. The other is *compromise*. Without them, no family can be happy. Compromise means "give and take." It means that sometimes you don't get everything you want. But no one ever does. That's why families need to compromise—so that each member gets some of what he or she wants. Cooperation means thinking about the other members of the family. It means considering their feelings. It means trying to make things work. It means working together.

A Stepfamily Is Not Like a First Family

Stepfamilies are different from first families. That is important to remember. (It does not mean they are better. It does not mean they are worse. It just means they are different.) How are they different?

○ Kids already exist.
In a first family the parents usually have some time together as a couple before they have children. They can get to know each other. They can be alone all the time. It is different in a stepfamily. There, you already exist. Your parents' relationship will be different. Your parents will have less privacy. And that can affect how the marriage grows.
A stepfamily is different from a first family for you too. A stepparent is not like a parent from birth. He or she is not someone you have known all your life. A stepparent is usually a stranger to you—and you to him or her.

○ Loyalties may be different.
There are no questions of loyalty in a first family. The father is the only father. The mother is the only mother. It is that way from the beginning. But stepfamilies are different. Often a natural parent is living. And that parent is not part of your new family. The question of loyalty arises. You may feel guilty about living in a family that does not include your absent parent. You may feel guilty even if that parent has died. You may still feel a strong connection to his or her memory.

○ Sense of belonging.
  In a first family it is easier to feel that you
  belong. There is one home. Both your parents
  are there. But in a stepfamily those feelings of
  belonging are not always there. Sometimes you
  must live in a new house in a new
  neighborhood. You have new relatives. These
  things often do not feel "real." You may not feel
  that you "belong" with these new things. You
  may feel that you belong in two different places.
  You cannot be sure whether your "real" home is
  with your mother or your father. Can that ever
  be decided? You do not want to feel that you
  belong in two places. You feel unhappy that
  way. You want to have one place that is home.

Problems with Names and Titles

Names are very important. They are important
in the world. They are important in families. What
we call a person shows how we feel about him or
her. Or how well we know the person. Names also
tell other people about relationships. They tell a
stranger who your parent is. They tell everyone
who *you* are.

In a stepfamily names can be a problem. Who
should use what last name? Should a stepchild take
a stepfather's name? Should a stepchild call her
stepmother "Mom"? These questions are not easy.
And they often cause children to feel
uncomfortable.

After a time, the stepparent can be called "Mom" or "Dad."

Dear Diary,
I am feeling very confused. My stepfather asked me today to call him "Daddy." Up to now I have called him "Robert." I don't think I want to call him "Daddy." I already have a daddy. I can't have two daddies. My stepbrother Bradford calls Robert "Daddy." But that's different. Robert *is* Bradford's real dad. But what do I do? If I can't call Robert "Daddy" he will think I don't love him. I do love him. But I want to call him "Robert." Is that so bad? I hope he understands.

Gretchen, age 14

Your stepparent may ask you to use "Mom" or "Dad." But this cannot be forced. You and your stepparent must both be comfortable with it. It must come from feelings of love and respect. And just like love and respect, if it is not natural, it will mean nothing. It will only make you and your stepparent uncomfortable.

> Dear Diary,
>   Today was my first Thanksgiving with Mom and Tony. We went to Tony's family's house. Tony's mom, my new "grandma" made lots of turkey. Tony embarrassed me. He introduced me to his cousins as "my wife's child, Gilberto." That made me feel bad. I thought we were all part of one big family now. I call Tony "Dad" sometimes. I love Tony. I wanted him to call me his son in front of other people. I wanted to feel like part of his family. I feel like Tony is ashamed of me in public.
>
>   Gilberto, age 14

All the members of your stepfamily should talk to each other about names. You need to speak openly and honestly. You need to tell each other what you want to be called. You may want to be called a son or a daughter. Or you may want to keep the title stepchild to show that you are not related naturally to the stepparent. Whatever is most comfortable is the best. No one should try to force a name or title.

Dear Diary,

I saw my daddy today. Then I came home. I saw my stepdad at home. I called him "Dad" too. I felt really bad. I felt like I was not being fair to my real dad. I should not call another man "Dad" if he is not my real dad. Even if Mom did marry him. I feel like I am being bad. My real dad would not want me to call my stepdad "Dad." But I love my stepdad too. I don't want to hurt either of my dads' feelings. Will I ever feel comfortable having two fathers?

Tina, age 13

You may feel that you are being disloyal to your natural parent if you call your stepparent "Mom" or "Dad." It is confusing. You love your natural parents. But you also love your stepparent. You must feel comfortable about calling your stepparent what he or she wants. There is nothing wrong with calling two people "Mom" or "Dad." It is okay if it feels okay. And it will feel okay if everyone talks about what they want to be called. That is why you and your parents should always discuss your feelings.

Changing Last Names

Many times stepchildren do not know what to do about last names. You may live with a natural parent and a stepparent. The natural parent may be your mother. She may change her name. She may take your stepfather's name. Then you are the only one with a different name. Some children like to take the stepfather's name. They want to feel like part of the new family. Or they want to have the same last name as their mother. But you do not have to change your name. You may feel that it is not your "real" name. You may feel uncomfortable about changing it. But you also feel "left out" of the family if you are the only one with a different name.

Remember What Names Really Are

Names are only signs. They tell something about you. But they do not tell about the person inside. Names tell other people who you are, not what you are. They are used to identify people. For instance, they tell a neighbor that you are "Ted Kurtz," the son of "Nathan Kurtz."

Many families like using two names. Some members have one last name. Others have a different last name. But they still feel like a family. This can be a good solution. It does not mean that the family is less of a family. It just means that people in the family have been in other families before.

Liz Thompson
19 Park Road
Watkins Glen, PA 14890

Domestic USA

Ms. Joan Smith-Stern
4056 Cedar Street
Rockville, MD. 20851

The Adoption Option

Some families feel that adoption of the children is a good idea. You may want to take your stepparent's name. Certain things become easier with adoption. You can use your parents' name at school. With adoption you are legally related to your stepparent. Adoption makes some children feel more secure. You may feel that you would be safe if something happened to your natural parent. If you were adopted you would still be legally united to your stepparent.

Sometimes adoption is best. It may be good when the other natural parent is dead, or very far away, or not regularly in touch. You may want to take another name if your other parent is not close or if you will never see him or her.

Unfair Expectations

Stepfamilies have many good points. People often spend too much time talking about the problems. They forget that a stepfamily can be a happy thing.

But unfair expectations happen when people think something will be better than it can be. Sometimes these are called "fixed ideas." They can cause a lot of unhappiness in stepfamilies. When people expect the family to be perfect, they are disappointed.

Stepparents cannot win love and trust with presents. It takes time
for these feelings to grow.

○ Expecting Instant Love.

Dear Diary,
   I feel bad. Dad just got married. To Donna. She's nice. But she's always asking me to go shopping with her. I like her but I have my own friends, too. And she is always saying "I love you." But I don't want her to say that. I hardly know her. And I feel like I am supposed to say I love her. But I don't. Not yet anyway. But she's my stepmom. Don't people expect me to love my own stepmother? Will I ever feel comfortable with Donna?

Sarah, age 14

Stepparents often want you to love them right away. They also want to love you right away. You may feel this as pressure. You may feel that you *have to* love your new parent right away. BUT IT IS OKAY IF YOU DON'T. It is not natural to force feelings. Especially feelings of love. If the stepfamily works out, the love may come of itself.

Most stepparents hardly know their stepchildren at first. How can they love them right away? Real love is based on respect and trust. These feelings take time to grow. And they cannot be forced.

Your stepparent may try too hard to win your love. This is often difficult for you. Your stepparent may think it will help to shower you with presents. Or to give you a lot of affection. But that is only putting more pressure on you. It is asking you to feel something you do not feel.

○ Thinking of Stepparents as "Replacement
   Parents."

> Dear Diary,
> Bob is acting strange. Ever since he moved in. He's
> always doing things for me. Like buying my favorite
> ice cream. And talking to me about sports. He keeps
> asking me what Dad is like. He keeps asking if Dad
> did things the same way he does them. I don't want
> Bob to try to be like Dad. My dad is special.
> Nobody can be like him. I just want Bob to be like
> Bob.
>
> Josh, age 13

Your stepparent may think that he or she should
replace your parent who has died or moved away.
He or she may try hard to be the same, to do the
same things. But no one can replace your parent.
No one should be expected to. Not even a
stepparent. Every parent is a unique person. Every
parent has strong points and weak points. No one
else in the world can copy or replace your parent.

Stepparents should be themselves. They should
be comfortable with giving their own strengths to a
new family. They should not ask you to think of
them as substitutes for your absent parent. And
you should not compare them to your other parent.

Stepparents should be thought of as additional
parents, not replacements.

○ Feeling That You Need to Forget the Absent
Parent.

Divorced parents often feel anger toward their
former spouse. They are often angry for a long
time. Because of this, you might be told to
forget your absent parent. Or maybe that parent
is never mentioned around the house. This is
what happens when one parent holds a grudge.
It is not fair to you.

You have loyalty and love for your absent
parent. Those feelings should always be respected.
Your feelings are separate. And they should not
be ignored.

The absent parent is often left out of plans. He
or she is forgotten at Christmas, Hanukkah, or
Thanksgiving. It can be very difficult to make
plans with one parent without the help of the
other. But when divorced parents are angry at each
other they do not cooperate. And then the children
suffer.

Name-calling

It is also hard for you to hear your parent speak
badly about your other (biological) parent. Name-
calling and blaming come from anger. They are
done to let out frustration (a feeling of
helplessness). But it is not your anger and
frustration. And you are upset when you hear it.
Parents have a right to be angry. But they must
understand that you may not share their anger.

Feeling Pushed Aside by Stepparents

Dear Diary

I am sick of having my stepmother around. I never
see my dad. I used to see him a lot before he
married her. He took me to the movies. And he
always took me for pizza afterward. He spent all his
free time with me. Those were the best days. But
now there is Margie. Now he spends all his time
with her. He says Margie needs time too. But I wish
she was not around. I feel like I lost both my
parents. And nobody pays any attention to me
anymore.

Paula, age 13

When parents remarry they feel that they are
starting over. But you feel it as a loss. You feel you
are losing the parent to someone else. You feel you
are losing your special place in the single-parent
family.

That may make you very angry. But you should
try to understand that marriage takes a lot of time.
Your parents arc working on a new life together.
When they are happy they can make a happy
family for you.

Expect Mixed Feelings

Every stepfamily starts with changes. They are
not necessarily bad. They are not necessarily good.
They are just different. We often assume that
"different" means "bad." But that is not true.
Changes are often for the better.

Chapter 3

When Parents Divorce

Stepfamilies used to be formed only after a parent died. Divorce was rare. Husbands and wives stayed together even if they were unhappy. They stayed together "for the sake of the children." When the children had grown up the parents might think about going their separate ways.

Today children do not prevent divorce. People think about divorce differently. It is now quite common to get a divorce.

Many children would like their parents to stay together no matter what. At least, they think they would. That is because it's easier to keep things the way they are. Change is almost always scary. But is it good to live in a family where the parents fight

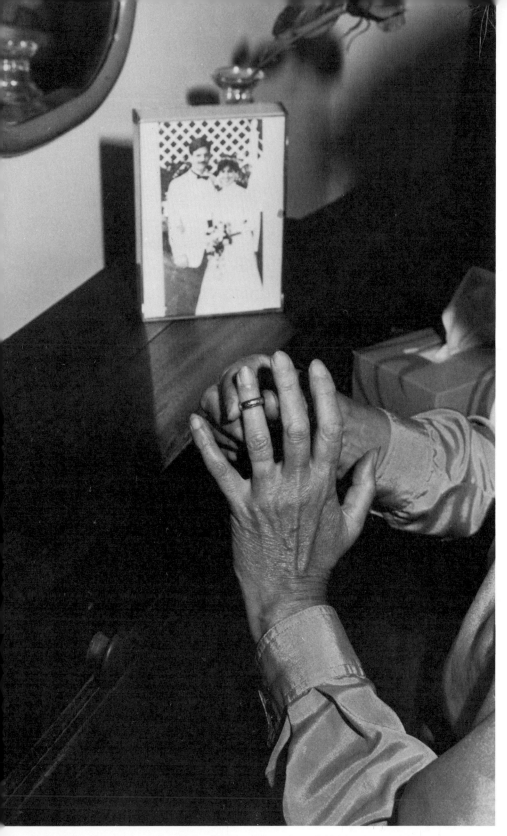

Parents divorce *each other*. It is never the children's fault.

all the time? Where everyone is unhappy? Or is it better to go through the pain of a divorce? To adjust to a new way of living. And to get on with your life?

Why Parents Divorce

Each divorce is as different as each marriage. But some things are alike. Parents give each other many common excuses. They often give excuses to their children as well. Here are some of the things that kids hear:

○ "You father/mother doesn't love me anymore."
○ "Your father/mother drinks too much."
○ "Your father/mother is mean to me."
○ "Your father/mother is mentally ill and not able to be happy with anyone."
○ "I am not getting what I need from my marriage."

Those are some of the feelings between husbands and wives who are thinking about divorce. Each excuse shows that one person thinks the other has changed. But the truth is that both people change. And sometimes the changes make it difficult for people to stay together.

Often jobs and new pressures change people. Sometimes a very sad event happens. That may change one person, or both. For whatever reason, the couple cannot live happily with each other anymore. They stop giving each other the things they need to be happy.

You Feel the Tension the Most

Unhappiness and tension ruin a family. They make each day uncomfortable. You all feel stress all the time. That puts you in a very difficult position. You cannot take sides because you love both parents. So you are in the middle.

> Dear Diary,
> Mom and Dad fight all the time. Every day. Every night. Sometimes I can't get to sleep. And I am too embarrassed to have friends over. I do not like to hear Mom and Dad call each other names. And I really feel uncomfortable when they ask me who is right. Nobody is right. I love them both. I can't say one is right and the other is wrong. That would be taking sides. I wish they would just go back to being happy, but I don't think that will happen. I used to like having dinner together. Now nobody talks. We just eat in silence. How can I be happy when people I love are unhappy?
>
> Clarence, age 16

When your parents fight it upsets everything. You count on your parents for many things. And those things are different when there is tension and anger in the house.

You need to rely on things being the same every day. You count on Mom or Dad to cook dinner every night. You depend on Mom or Dad to drive you to tennis practice. And you need Mom and

Knowing they can depend on their parents makes children feel secure.

When parents argue, children often feel afraid and confused.

Dad to have free time to spend with you. But when a marriage has problems all of those things can change. And that causes much pain and anger for you.

Trying to Hide Conflict

Your parents may try to hide their troubles from you. They think that if the family looks happy they will all *be* happy. They try to act happy. Then one day, without warning, it all blows up at once. It hits you suddenly. Then you are angry and shocked. You may not even believe it.

Your parents' troubles may be so bad that they can't be hidden. But you may still try to ignore them. You may pretend they don't exist. It is too painful for you to think about what might happen.

Divorce May Be the Best Answer

Divorce is not always a bad thing. When a marriage just does not work, it should be ended. That is often hard to accept at first. But in the long run it is best.

Sometimes you and your mother are being beaten or abused. Or you may just be threatened. Either way, separation and divorce may be needed.

Many people see divorce as a way to end unhappiness. But the decision is never easy. It is always hard to think about changing your life. But change may be best.

You Need to Know about the Divorce

It is very hard for your parents to tell you they are going to be divorced. They know you will meet the news with tears and begging. You will be frightened. You will be angry too. You may offer bribes to your parents. You may try to make a deal. You may promise to be good if the parents stay together. But your behavior cannot keep a marriage together.

You may get into a panic about moving. Maybe you will be upset about losing friends and changing schools. Most of all, you will be scared about losing a parent when one moves out.

Still, your parents should tell you what is happening. They should not let divorce drop suddenly like a bomb one day. Your parents should let you know what to expect. That way, you will not fear the worst. You will see that it's not the end of life. By explaining the divorce to you, your parents let you know that they are thinking about you too. Not just themselves.

When you are not told what is going on or what to expect, you may imagine things on your own. You may have a completely wrong idea about the reason for the divorce. You may think it's because Dad had trouble holding a job. Or maybe it was because Mom wanted to go back to school. Even worse, you may think it was something *you* did. That is why it is best for your parents to let you know as much as possible.

Moving away can be a frightening experience for a child.

Parents Divorce Each Other, Not Their Children

Your parents are not going to divorce because of you. Parents divorce because *they* have problems. They may have problems with each other. Or they may have problems with themselves. You may feel that your parents are rejecting you. You may think that you haven't been "good enough." But that is not true. No child can prevent a parent from feeling unhappy in a bad marriage.

Common Fears and Emotions

Dear Diary,
Yesterday Mom told me she was going to divorce Dad. They have yelled at each other a lot. This last week was very bad. They never stopped yelling. I am scared. Mom says Dad is moving away. He's moving to another state. He is leaving us alone. I am afraid I will never see him again. I hate him. I hate them both. Now we won't have any money. And I won't be able to go out with my friends anymore. If we have to move I will die. I hate moving. I don't want to leave my friends. I don't want this to happen.

Michelle, age 15

These are very common fears. You will probably have some of them. And you will need to tell your parents about the fears.

Remarriage and Change

It is never easy when a parent remarries. The new marriage can be upsetting for a number of reasons. For you, remarriage ends a dream. You had hoped that your natural parents would get back together. Anger often comes when a dream is ended. That is why remarriage is often met with anger.

Remarriage also changes your relationship to your parents. You are already torn between your natural parents. Now a third parent is added, and perhaps another child. And that means a whole new set of feelings. And a whole new set of problems.

Maybe you do not trust new relationships. You have already lost one parent. That makes it hard to trust parents. And it makes it hard to trust adults. Especially stepparents. You may stop trusting anybody. Maybe you feel you have been let down by your parents. And you think, "If I can't trust my natural parents, how can I trust my stepparent?"

You may use your anger to make your stepfamily unhappy. Stepparents are easy targets for anger. You may make things hard for your stepparent. You may misbehave. You may not cooperate. You hope your parent will give up. Then maybe your parent will go back to the old family.

Maybe you do not feel comfortable in your new stepfamily. You may think it feels "fake."

When a Family Changes after a Death

I t takes many things to make a stepfamily work. But one thing is the most important of all. The family members must understand each other's feelings. Each member must see what makes the stepfamily special. Then each member can understand the special feelings involved. Talking openly is always best. Discussing feelings is the best way to solve problems. It is also the best way to avoid problems.

Something has to happen before a stepfamily begins. A family changes or ends. The breakup of a family is very painful for all its members. A first family is not forgotten just because a stepfamily begins. It takes time to get used to the loss of a

41

first family. It takes time to adjust. You cannot be happy until you have adjusted to the loss.

When a Parent Dies

Stepfamilies are often formed after the death of a parent. Sometimes the surviving parent raises the children alone. This is called a single-parent family. Often the parent remarries after the death of the other parent.

The greatest loss for you is the loss of a parent. Your parents are the most important people in your life. Parents offer love. They give security. Parents give you a feeling of stability. That means that you can rely on things staying the same. Stability is very important.

A parent teaches you how to act. A parent shows that when you give love, you get love in return. This is a basic part of living. A parent is also a role model to teach you how to behave. You learn how to act by watching your parents.

Parents give you a feeling of security. Sometimes you feel scared. You become frightened about the future. It is important for you to know that someone will protect you.

The whole family is greatly disturbed when a parent dies. The daily routine in the family ends. There is no more Sunday brunch with the whole family together. There is no one to give you driving lessons. Nothing is as it used to be.

When a parent dies, family life changes very suddenly.

Feeling Guilty

> Dear Diary,
>   This is the first day I can write in my diary again.
> I stopped writing because my dad died. He was
> killed in a car accident. It happened two weeks ago.
> I have been crying for the last two weeks straight.
> Mom has been crying too. And so has my sister,
> Jenny. I cannot stop thinking about Dad. His things
> are everywhere in the house. Like his chair at the
> dining room table. I asked Mom not to take his chair
> away. She said she wouldn't. I don't get why Dad
> got killed. He was the best driver. He was always
> strong. I feel bad that sometimes I upset him.
> Sometimes I think that maybe he was upset when he
> got killed. I think maybe I made it happen. I wish I
> had never made him angry. The day before he got
> killed he yelled at me. It was for not keeping my
> room clean. I don't think I can ever stop seeing Dad
> in my head. I keep seeing him the way he was. I
> wish he was still here. I am angry at him for going
> away. He left me and Mom and Jenny alone.
>
> Gary, age 14

You may feel guilty when a parent dies. You feel
that maybe you caused the death. You think you
did it by upsetting your parent. You also wish you
had behaved better when your parent was alive.
People cannot control death. Death is not caused
by anyone's behavior. Most teenagers feel that they

could have been better children for their parents. It is a natural feeling. With time, you will realize that your parent loved you. You remember how your parent was happy with you. You realize that you were loved for your good points and bad points together.

Time to Mourn

The death of a parent is one of the most upsetting things that will ever happen to you. It takes a lot of time to get over that. You need time to be sad. Feeling sad about a person's dying is called "mourning." Often a part of mourning is feeling angry with your dead parent for leaving. Another part of it is deep sadness because you can never see your parent again. Still another part of mourning is adjusting to change. When your parent dies life becomes very difficult. Almost everything changes.

Becoming Part of a Stepfamily

For a stepfamily to work, all members must understand the others. They must understand what has happened. They must respect each other's feelings. They must understand what other members are going through. They must also cooperate. A stepfamily can be happy only when the parents and the children understand one another.

Dear Diary,
Everybody wants me to look happy all the time. Dad
is always telling me to smile. Mostly when we are
with my grandparents. But I don't feel like smiling.
I don't feel happy. Mom has only been dead for
eight months. I miss her. I feel like crying all the
time. But Dad says Paula will think I'm not happy
with our new family. People will think I don't like
Paula. She's my new stepmother. I like her all right.
But she will never replace my mom. I don't know
why Dad married her. Didn't he love Mom as much
as we do?

Laurie, age 15

People often want children to act a certain way
when a stepfamily begins. Parents want to make
the family work right away. They want everyone to
be happy. They are eager for everyone to love
everyone else right away. But those are not fair
expectations to have.

Often unfair things are asked of you. You are
asked to act in ways that are hard when you are
mourning the death of a parent. Here are some
unfair things that you may be asked.

○ Stop frowning. It's over. Try to forget it.
A parent may ask you to try to forget what
happened so that the new family can be
"happy." But that is too hard for you. You can't
just stop feeling sadness. Sadness is a natural
feeling. It can't just be turned off. It must stop
over time.

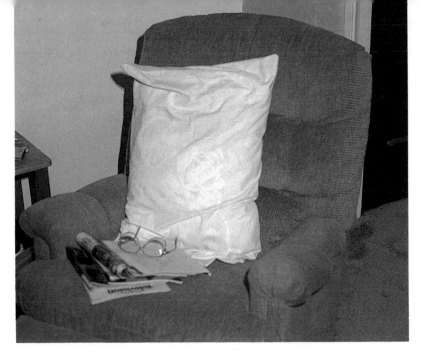

There will always be reminders of a missing parent.

- Stop crying. Be a man. Try to be grown up. Sometimes your parent will ask you to stop *showing* sadness. That is also hard. Crying and feeling sad is a very important part of letting go. It is part of getting used to a loss. Parents may want everything about a new family to seem perfect. They don't want to see crying or unhappiness. But feeling the pain of a death should never be avoided.

- What's wrong with you? You don't seem to care. Sometimes your parent may think you aren't crying *enough*. Your parent feels pain and wants you to feel the same way. Then he or she may say you don't care. That makes you feel guilty. But everybody deals with pain and death differently. Some people cry for months. Others do not cry at all. Others only cry in the privacy of their bedroom. All of those ways are okay.

47

○ Don't talk that way about your father. He's
   dead.
   You may want to talk about your dead parent. It
   helps you to accept the fact that the parent is
   gone. You need to say out loud that you are
   angry about the parent's leaving. Or maybe that
   the parent was "dumb" for getting killed. Some
   people think that doesn't show respect for the
   dead. But talking like that helps you remember
   that even your dead parent had faults. He or she
   is not perfect just because of being dead. When
   you accept that the dead person was not perfect,
   you are coping with the death normally.

Unfair expectations like these make it harder for
you to accept the loss you feel. They prevent you
from dealing naturally with the death of your
parent. Mourning must be completed naturally.
Without that, you cannot accept a stepparent.

When a Widowed Parent Remarries

A woman whose husband dies is called a widow.
A husband whose wife dies is a widower. Parents
who lose a husband or wife sometimes want to
marry again, especially if they have children. You
may be unhappy when your parent remarries. You
may have many uncomfortable feelings.

Your surviving parent becomes closer to you
when the other parent is gone. He or she loves,
cares for, and protects you even more than before.

Things a Parent Cannot Get from You

Many of your parent's needs you cannot fill. Even all your love and friendship are not enough. Your parent may feel lonely for other adults. Adults have feelings that you cannot understand. They have emotions that they cannot share with you.

Parents are likely to miss love and sex. Love and sex are very important for adults to share. Parents need closeness with other adults. They also need to feel attractive to others. They have been living without a husband or wife. Soon they may need to get back into the world, to feel that they are "still alive."

Most parents handle these feelings by starting to have dates. If they find someone they care about, they may want to remarry.

A Stepparent Is Not a Replacement

When your parent does remarry, your new stepparent may want to be a replacement for your dead parent. This is never a good idea. It is unfair to ask you to think of a stranger as a replacement for your natural parent. He or she cannot be replaced by anyone. You have strong ties to your natural parent. These cannot and should not be forgotten.

It is much better for you to think of a stepparent as an added parent. It is better for stepparents to think of themselves that way too.

Loneliness and Hurt

You probably feel very alone when your parent remarries. You feel that your natural parent has joined forces with the stepparent. You may feel left out. You may feel that "It's me against them." You may also feel that you have no one to talk to. You feel that your natural parent won't want to hear your feelings about the stepparent. That makes it hard for you to speak truthfully. Especially if you don't have only nice things to say.

Feeling Remarriage as Betrayal

You may feel that your parent is betraying your other parent by remarrying. You may feel this even if the other natural parent is dead. You will be angry with the surviving parent for giving love to someone else. You may even feel that the stepparent has stolen the love that the other natural parent deserves. But you can't tell your parent whom to love. You must accept the fact that your parent will love other people.

A Stepparent Can Also Be a Hero

A stepparent can often be a real hero. She or he can make a child and a parent feel like a whole family again. A stepparent can provide the "missing piece" that is needed to complete a family picture. He or she can provide security and love. And a stepparent can meet the needs of the other parent. These roles are worthy of respect and love.

Chapter 5

Living with Stepbrothers and Stepsisters

Having stepsiblings (stepbrothers and stepsisters) has good points as well as bad. It is like any other part of living in a family. There are always rough spots between brothers and sisters in a natural family, even in the best times. But added trouble can come when children are thrown together after their parents marry.

We have talked about many problems with stepchildren and stepparents. We have talked about people expecting love right away. And expecting other changes too fast. These expectations can also cause problems between stepsiblings. It takes time for you to get used to each other's habits. It takes time to know each other well enough to like each other. Sometimes one sibling feels pushed aside by the one who has moved into his or her home.

Sharing a room with a new stepsibling is hard. It takes time to get used to one another.

Jealousy

Stepsibs can become jealous of each other.
Sometimes they are jealous of the attention their
own parent gives a stepsib. Sometimes there is
competition for a "special" place in the family.
Who is the best in school? Who is the best in
sports? There is always competition between
brothers and sisters. Natural siblings have
problems getting along too. Sometimes the
competition is healthy. It makes some people try
harder than they might otherwise.

Different Children, Different Attitudes

Parents may treat one child as the "natural"
child and the other as the "stepchild." They
probably don't mean to do that. But they need
time to adjust to the new family as well. It may
take time before the parents see each of you
children equally. Some favoring cannot be avoided.
Each parent has lived with his or her own child
much longer. He or she is more sensitive to that
child. It cannot be helped. Each may favor that
child without even knowing it.

You may have to learn new rules. Old rules may
not apply in the new family.

Gaining Stepsiblings Can Be a Good Thing

Many children are happy to gain new brothers
and sisters. Getting stepsibs has many good points.

Here are some of them:

○ A stepsibling means a new friendship.
  Sometimes it means the end of being alone.
  Stepsibs of similar ages are new companions.

○ A stepsib is someone who shares the stepfamily
  experience. He or she understands the problems
  of being a stepchild. A stepsib knows what you
  are going through. You can go through the
  family adjustments together.

○ Stepsibs can help each other understand
  stepparents. Each can explain his or her natural
  parent to the other. This can bring about a
  better relationship for all the members of the
  family. Communication will be better too.

○ When stepsibs get together they can share. They
  can share friends, toys, clothes, and many other
  things. This is often a great boost to both
  stepsibs.

Stepsibs Who Visit

Visiting stepsiblings can be a problem. This is
usually because they are not around so much. You
simply have less time to work things out.

A visiting stepsib may resent the live-in stepsib.
She or he may be jealous because the live-in
stepchild spends more time with the natural parent.
Visiting stepsibs are also unsure of themselves.
They are unsure of how their real parent and the
new parent feel about them. They do not feel they
are part of the family they are visiting.

A New Child for the Remarried Parents

Many remarried couples want to have children. They want to have a child created by them together. Some feel that a new child will "cement" their marriage. Some feel that having a baby will celebrate the relationship.

A New Baby and a Single Stepchild

When there is only one child in a stepfamily a new baby can cause some uncomfortable feelings. The stepchild can feel ignored. It may seem that the new baby gets all the attention.

The stepchild may feel that the baby is "more related" to the family and that he or she is "less related" and less loved. A stepchild can feel left out of the family that way. That is why the new parents should take extra care to show their love to both children.

Maybe you confuse blood relationship with love. You forget that a blood relationship does not make someone love you any more or less.

A New Baby and Loneliness

Newborn babies need a lot of attention. They take up most of a parent's time. You could be jealous of a newborn sibling. You could feel ignored and unloved. But parents can love more than one child at a time.

Teens and parents should discuss their feelings with each other.

Chapter 6

Teens in Stepfamilies

T eens are also called "adolescents." An adolescent is a person between the ages of 11 and 21. That is a very hard time to become a stepchild.

In adolescence you are looking for your own identity. You begin to form personal relationships outside your family. You often feel awkward.

This is also a time when you have problems with your parents. Adolescents want to feel independent. But parents do not want to give you too much freedom at once. Often adolescents want more freedom than parents are willing to give.

Becoming a stepchild in your teens is very difficult. It is a time when you want to be alone. Or with friends your age. But the new family want you to be a part of their group. They want you to spend time with the family. This can create tension between your parents and you.

You have to adapt to new rules when a stepfamily is formed. This can be very frustrating. Often you have just accepted the rules of the first family. You have just learned to deal with the old ways. Now the game changes. Things seem to be starting from scratch.

A Time of More Emotional Maturity

As a teenager you know more about relationships than small children do. You understand the possible problems between people. You can see your parents more clearly. You see that they are not perfect. You see that they have many problems. And you do not blame yourself for your parent's problems.

You may feel angry that you do not have a united family to support you. Your own problems are bad enough. Having family problems can seem too much to bear.

You need to keep your expectations fair. Talking to other members of the family can help you do that. Parents are not perfect. They make mistakes. They can be unfair. They can expect things of you that are not fair. Parents need to hear from you. They can learn about feelings too.

Family members must talk to each other honestly. They must be open about their feelings. Then no one will have unfair expectations.

Glossary—Explaining New Words

abuse   Hurting someone else.

adolescence   Time from age eleven to age twenty-one.

adoption   Becoming the legal child of another person.

biological   Having to do with the body; natural.

competition   Rivalry; trying to win a contest.

compromise   Agreement by meeting someone halfway.

conflict   Having problems with someone.

confusion   State of being mixed up.

cooperation   Working together with other people.

courage   Bravery; strength to meet problems.

crisis   Emergency situation.

disappoint   To frustrate; to let down.

discipline   Training in good behavior.

divorce   Legal ending of marriage.

embarrassment   Feeling of discomfort, shame.

emotional   Having strong feelings.

expectations   What people think will happen.

favoritism   Treating one person better than others.

frustration   Feeling upset, discouraged.

grudge   Long-lasting feeling of anger at someone.

guidance   Showing someone the way.

guilt   Feeling of being responsible for something.

identity   Who a person is.

imagine   To have a mental picture.

jealousy   Feeling that someone else has something better.

loyalty   Being true to a person.

mourning   Feeling sad about a death.

privacy   The right to be alone.

rejection   Not being wanted.

relation   Member of the same family.

replacement   Something that takes the place of something else.

resent   Dislike; feel jealous of.

respect   Looking up to a person.

role model   Person whose behavior is an example to others.

security   Feeling of being safe.

sensitive   Aware of the way others feel.

separation   Moving apart.

sex   Lovemaking; male-female behavior.

sibling   Brother or sister.

single-parent family   Family with only one parent.

stepfamily   Members of two families joined in one new family.

stepparent   Parent related by marriage but not by blood.

stepsibling   Brother or sister related by marriage but not by blood.

title   Formal name.

unique   Being the only one.

weapon   Something used to hurt another person.

wholeness   Feeling of being complete.

widow   Wife whose husband has died.

widower   Husband whose wife has died.

Where To Go For Help

STEPFAMILY FOUNDATION
333 West End Avenue
New York, NY 10023
Telephone: (212) 877-3244

STEPFAMILY ASSOCIATION OF AMERICA
28 Allegheny Avenue
Suite 1307
Baltimore, MD 21204
Telephone: (301) 823-7570

AMERICAN ASSOCIATION FOR MARRIAGE
AND FAMILY THERAPY
1717 K Street NW
Room 407
Washington, DC 20006
Telephone: (202) 429-1825

NATIONAL COUNCIL ON FAMILY
RELATIONS
1910 West County Road B
St. Paul, MN 55113
Telephone: (612) 633-6933

For Further Reading

Berger, Terry. *Stepchild*. New York: Messner, 1980, 63 pages. This book is about the thoughts and feelings of a boy whose mother remarries. It discusses the problems and adjustments involved in being part of a stepfamily.

Berry, Joy. *Every Kid's Guide to Understanding Parents*. Chicago, IL: Children's Press. 1986. This book teaches children about why parents do what they do and about how to get along in a family.

Kaplan, Leslie S. *Coping with Stepfamilies*. New York: Rosen Publishing Company, 1986. This book examines stepfamilies in detail. It discusses some of the problems that can arise in stepfamilies and how to deal with them.

Masoli, Lisa Ann. *Things to Know About Death and Dying*. Morristown, NJ: Silver Burdett Press, 1987. This book about death and dying, also discusses stepfamilies formed after the death of a biological parent.

Raible, H. "The Stepsibling Shuffle." *Choices*, September 1987, pages 14–17. This article discusses some of the problems that can arise in a stepfamily.

Index

About the Author
Bruce Glassman has authored five books for young adults and has
been a staff writer on two Connecticut newspapers. At present he lives
in New York City where he is an editor of journalism and history
books.

About the Editor
Evan Stark is a well-known sociologist, educator, and therapist
as well as a popular lecturer on women's and children's health issues.
Dr. Stark was the Henry Rutgers Fellow at Rutgers University, an as
sociate at the Institution for Social and Policy Studies at Yale University, and a Fulbright Fellow at the University of Essex. He is the author
of many publications in the field of family relations and is the father of
four children.

Acknowledgments and Photo Credits
P. 2, 8, 13, 14, 33, 34/35, 43, 52, 56, Stuart Rabinowitz; p. 19, 24, 30, 38,
47, Blackbirch Graphics.

Design/Production: Blackbirch Graphics, Inc.
Cover Photograph: Stuart Rabinowitz